LOOKING AT OUR LIVES

PICTURE DICTIONARY

STUDENT WORKBOOK

KAREN CARLISI   **ROBIN STEVENS**

EECI INC.

CREDITS

Library of Congress Catalog-in-Publication Data

Carlisi, K.

Looking At Our Lives Picture Dictionary Workbook / Karen Carlisi, Robin Stevens.

1. Picture Dictionaries. English.
2. English language. Textbooks for foreign speakers.

ISBN 0-9649379-1-3

Remen-Willis Design Group

Ann Remen-Willis, Design Director

Siri Weber Feeney, Design

David Kirby, Cover Design

Illustration: Unit 1 D.J. Simison, Unit 2 Doug Roy, Unit 3 Jane McCreary, Unit 4 Martha Weston, Unit 5 D.J. Simison, Unit 6 Siri Weber Feeney, Len Epstein, Unit 7 James Buckley, Unit 8 Susan Jaekel, Unit 9 Doug Roy, Unit 10 Deborah Morse. All FM/RM and Dialogue boxes D.J. Simison. Cover D.J. Simison, Len Epstein.

CONTENTS

USING THE WORKBOOK

The workbook for *Looking At Our Lives Picture Dictionary* is designed for practice and reinforcement of the vocabulary presented in the dictionary. The workbook provides an opportunity to learn the target vocabulary items through writing exercises, listening and speaking activities, pronunciation practice, and a short grammar focus.

Each workbook unit contains four different activity sections: "Word Power," "Grammar Box," "Listening In," and "Looking at Your Life." The units are designed so that the sequential use of these activity sections reinforces what is learned in a previous section and encourages integration of skills. The sections are described below:

WORD POWER The exercises in this section will help students to learn the vocabulary, with focus on picture identification, meaning, and spelling. Some of the exercises are:

Write the Picture Word-picture identification to reinforce word-referent correspondence.

Word Scramble Scrambled words to practice spelling of vocabulary items.

Spell It! Words with missing letters for spelling practice.

Matching Matching for word-picture identification, meaning, or parts of vocabulary items.

Word Groups Emphasis on meaning through classification of target vocabulary into groups.

GRAMMAR BOX A brief grammar point is presented and practiced in each unit. The grammar box addresses a specific grammar focus related to the use of the target vocabulary. There is a short fill-in-the blank exercise following the grammar box to practice the grammar point.

LISTEN IN This section helps to develop recognition and comprehension skills for the target vocabulary. The exercises in this section encourage students to identify words through pictures as they hear them as well as to understand them in the context of a conversation. Some of the exercises in this section are:

Listen and Point Students point to the picture in the dictionary to identify the words as they listen to the tape.

Listen and Check This is a task-based exercise in which students listen to a conversation and check target vocabulary on a list or chart as it applies to the situation.

Listen and Choose A comprehension exercise in which students choose the correct answer to a question about a conversation or text they've heard on the tape.

Listen and Write A dictation exercise which encourages spelling practice.

Listen and Decide A true-false comprehension exercise based on the conversation or text on the tape.

LOOKING AT YOUR LIFE This section gives students an opportunity to practice using the vocabulary to communicate about the theme of the unit. There are two different activities:

Draw and Tell Students draw something from their personal experience as it relates to the theme of the unit. The drawing is then used as a stimulus for oral interaction which incorporates the vocabulary from the unit.

Write It! Each unit ends with this section which provides practice writing the words and using them in a context related to the theme of the unit and the personal experience of the student.

UNIT 1: OUR SCHOOL
PART 1   THE CLASSROOM   Pages 6–7
Word Power

Do you have a **pencil sharpener**?
Yes, I do.

Write the Picture

Look at the pictures. Write the words.

Example: Do you have a _____*ruler*_____?

1. Do you have a _____?

2. Do you have a _____?

3. Do you have a _____?

4. Do you have a _____?

5. Do you have some _____?

6. Do you have an _____?

7. Do you have a _____?

6 UNIT 1 / *LOOKING AT OUR LIVES Picture Dictionary*

Word Scramble

Unscramble the words.

Example: rceladna _c_ _a_ _l_ _e_ _n_ _d_ _a_ _r_

1. ractehe _t_ ___ ___ ___ ___ ___ ___

2. nilecp _p_ ___ ___ ___ ___ ___

3. rnbdei _b_ ___ ___ ___ ___ ___

4. lcahk _c_ ___ ___ ___ ___

Listen In

Listen and Point

Look at pages 6–7 in your *Picture Dictionary*. Listen to the tape.
Point to your picture as you listen.

Listen and Check

Listen to the tape again. Check off the words when you hear them.

1. teacher _____

2. blackboard _____

3. bulletin board _____

4. computer _____

5. clock _____

6. abacus _____

7. globe _____

8. notebook _____

9. pencil _____

10. paintbrush _____

PART 2   USING SCHOOL EQUIPMENT   Pages 8–9

Word Power
Spell It!

Fill in the missing letters. Then write the words.

Example: *sl__i__ __d__ e proje__c__ __t__ or*   _____ *slide projector* _____

1. cal ____ ____ lator   _____

2. comput ____ ____   _____

3. vid ____ ____ tap ____   _____

4. ear ____ ____ ones   _____

5. ____ ____ inter   _____

Eyes, Fingers, and Ears

Look at the pictures. Circle the words that match the pictures.

Example:

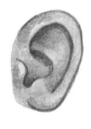

(*overhead projector*)

tape recorder

computer

1. monitor

   earphones

   keyboard

2. printer

   tape recorder

   calculator

Is there a **computer** in your classroom?
Yes, there is.

Speak Out!

Look at the pictures. Use the dialogue box. Ask your partner.

1.

2.

3.

4.

5.

Listen In

Listen and Check

Listen to the questions. Check off the equipment in Anna's classroom.

Example: Do you have a slide projector in your classroom?
            Yes, I do.

            slide projector _____ ✓

1. calculator _____

2. VCR _____

3. overhead projector _____

4. computer _____

5. earphones _____

6. printer _____

7. tape recorder _____

8. television _____

9. clock _____

PART 3 VERBS Pages 10–11
Word Power

What is Susan doing?
She's **drawing a picture**.

Write the Picture

Look at the pictures. Write the answers. Practice with your partner.

Example: What is Bobby doing? He's _____*closing his book*_____ .

1. What is Susan doing? She's _____

    _____ .

2. What is Jim doing? He's _____

    _____ .

3. What is Pam doing? She's _____

    _____ .

4. What is Anna doing? She's _____

    _____ .

5. What is David doing? He's _____

    _____ .

Listen In

Listen and Choose

Listen and choose the correct answer.

Example: What is Susan doing? ____*a*____

        a. She's opening her book.

        b. She's closing her book.

1. What is Anna doing? _____

    a. She's turning on the printer.

    b. She's watching a video.

2. What is the teacher doing? _____

    a. He's erasing the board.

    b. He's answering a question.

3. What is Tom doing? _____

    a. He's reading a book.

    b. He's raising his hand.

4. What is Jim doing? _____

    a. He's taking out a piece of paper.

    b. He's taking a test.

5. What is Bobby doing? _____

    a. He's drawing a picture.

    b. He's writing his name.

6. What is Kate doing? _____

    a. She's standing up.

    b. She's sitting down.

Grammar Box

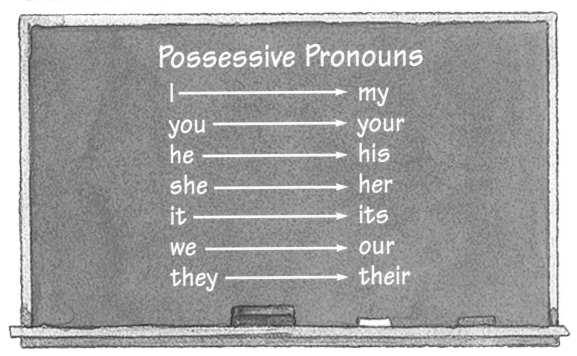

Fill in the Blanks

Fill in the blank with a possessive pronoun.

Example: I am turning on the printer.

There's a printer in _____*my*_____ classroom.

1. <u>He</u> is listening to an audiotape.

   He has a tape recorder in _____ classroom.

2. <u>They</u> are using the computer.

   There's a computer in _____ classroom.

3. <u>We</u> are watching a videotape.

   We have a VCR in _____ classroom.

4. <u>She</u> is using a transparency.

   There's an overhead projector in _____ classroom.

Looking at Your Life
Draw and Tell

Draw a picture of your classroom. Draw the people and things in your classroom. Use the words from this unit. Tell your partner about your classroom.

My Classroom

Write It!

Look at your picture from "Draw and Tell". Write about your classroom.
Use the vocabulary and verbs on pages 6–11 of your *Picture Dictionary*.

About My Classroom

This is my classroom. There's a/an/some _____,

a/an/some _____, and

a/an/some _____ in my classroom.

The teacher is _____.

One student is _____.

Another student is _____.

I am _____.

UNIT 2: THINGS WE LEARN
PART 1   NUMBERS   Pages 12–13

Word Power
Write the Picture

Look at pages 12–13 in your picture dictionary. Write the words for the numbers.

Example: 5 _____ *five* _____

1. 11 _____

2. 14 _____

3. 100,000 _____

4. 50 _____

5. 12 _____

6. 300 _____

7. 15 _____

8. 80 _____

9. 2 _____

16   UNIT 2 / *LOOKING AT OUR LIVES Picture Dictionary*

Did Tom win the race?
No, he was **third**.

Fill in the Blanks

Look at the cardinal numbers. Write the ordinal numbers in the blanks.

Example: 5 _____*fifth*_____

1. 8 _____

2. 4 _____

3. 2 _____

4. 6 _____

5. 1 _____

6. 3 _____

7. 7 _____

8. 10 _____

9. 9 _____

Write the Numbers

Read the words. Write the numbers.

Example: seven hundred _____700_____

1. ten thousand _____

2. three _____

3. eighteen _____

4. four hundred _____

5. ninety _____

6. one billion _____

7. thirteen _____

8. ten _____

9. seventy _____

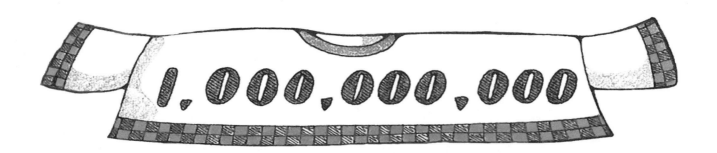

Listen In
Listen and Write

Listen to the words. Write the numbers. Then spell the words for the numbers.

Example:

Numbers	Words
700	*seven hundred*

Numbers	Words
1. _____	_____
2. _____	_____
3. _____	_____
4. _____	_____
5. _____	_____
6. _____	_____
7. _____	_____
8. _____	_____
9. _____	_____
10. _____	_____

PART 2 MATHEMATICS Pages 14–15

Word Power

Matching

Find the mathematical terms.
Write the letters on the lines.

Example: 3 – 1 = 2 _____*c*_____

1. 30% _____

2. 2 + x = 3 _____

3. 2 x 4 = 8 _____

4. 1/6, 1/8 _____

5. width, radius _____

6. 0.3 _____

7. 6 ÷ 3 = 2 _____

a. fractions

b. division

c. ***subtraction***

d. geometry

e. percentage

f. multiplication

g. decimals

h. algebra

Student Workbook

Word Scramble

Unscramble the words.

1. tbsuratc _s_ ___ ___ ___ ___ ___ ___ ___

2. idevdi _d_ ___ ___ ___ ___ ___

3. tilpumly _m_ ___ ___ ___ ___ ___ ___ ___

4. slamiedc _d_ ___ ___ ___ ___ ___ ___ ___

5. brgalea _a_ ___ ___ ___ ___ ___ ___

Make a Choice

Read the mathematical terms. Write an example.

Example: addition _____ *8 + 4 = 12* _____

1. multiplication _____

2. subtraction _____

3. percentage _____

4. fractions _____

5. algebra _____

6. decimals _____

Bobby, can you do the **addition** exercise?
Yes, **twenty–three plus six equals twenty–nine.**

Got It!

Read the question. Use the correct math words to answer the questions.

Example: Can you do the multiplication exercise?   2 x 31 = 62

Yes, _____*two times thirty–one equals sixty–two*_____

1. Can you do the division exercise?   72 ÷ 6 = 12

Yes, _____

2. Can you do the subtraction exercise?   61 – 15 = 46

Yes, _____

3. Can you do the addition exercise?   7 + 13 = 20

Yes, _____

Listen In

Listen and Choose

Listen to the mathematics problem. Circle the name of the correct mathematical term.

1.   addition   multiplication

2.   subtraction   division

3.   fractions   percentage

4.   algebra   geometry

5.   decimals   division

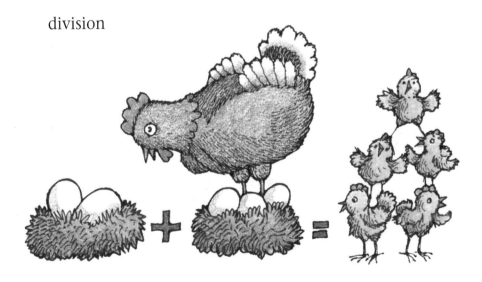

Listen and Write

Listen to the numbers. Write the mathematics.

Example: _____ *2 x 31 = 62* _____

1. _____

2. _____

3. _____

4. _____

5. _____

6. _____

7. _____

8. _____

Grammar Box

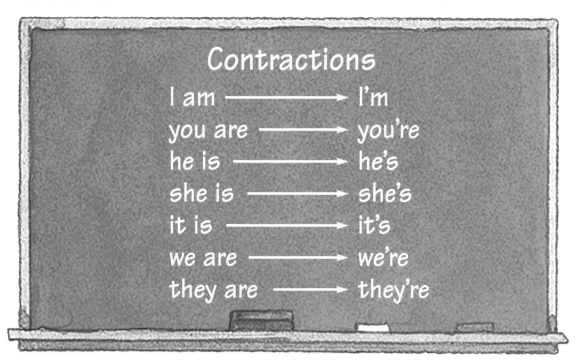

Contractions

I am ⟶ I'm
you are ⟶ you're
he is ⟶ he's
she is ⟶ she's
it is ⟶ it's
we are ⟶ we're
they are ⟶ they're

Change It!

Read the sentences. Rewrite the sentences using a contraction.

Example: <u>I am</u> doing division.   *I'm doing division.*

1. <u>It is</u> an oval.

   _____

2. <u>She is</u> doing subtraction.

   _____

3. <u>They are</u> fourth.

   _____

4. <u>We are</u> doing algebra.

   _____

PART 3   SHAPES AND COLORS   Pages 16–17

Word Power
Write the Picture

Look at the pictures. Write the words for the shapes.

Example: _____*oval*_____

1

1. _____

2

2. _____

3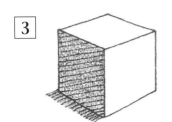

3. _____

4

4. _____

5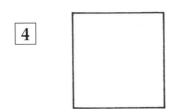

5. _____

Student Workbook

6

6. _____

7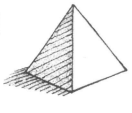

7. _____

8 ⬤

8. _____

9

9. _____

Spell It!

Fill in the missing letters. Then write the words.

1. ___ r ___ ___ n g ___ ___   _____

2. ___ i r ___ l ___   _____

3. s ___ ___ a r ___   _____

4. ___ l a ___ ___   _____

5. ___ ___ r p ___ e   _____

Listen In

What shape is an egg?
It's an **oval**.

Listen and Write

Listen to the tape. Write the shapes or colors.

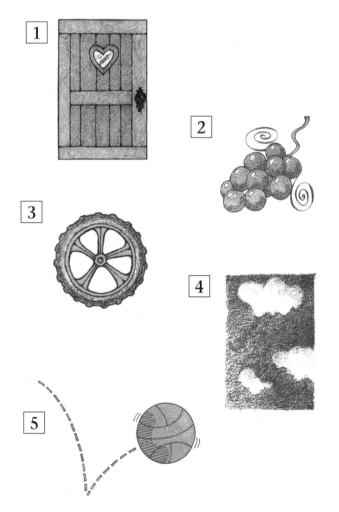

1. What shape is a door?

   It's a _____.

2. What color are grapes?

   They're _____.

3. What shape is a wheel?

   It's a _____.

4. What color is the sky?

   It's _____.

5. What shape is a basketball?

   It's a _____.

Student Workbook

Looking at Your Life

Draw and Tell

Draw four shapes. Make each shape a different color. Tell your partner about your pictures.

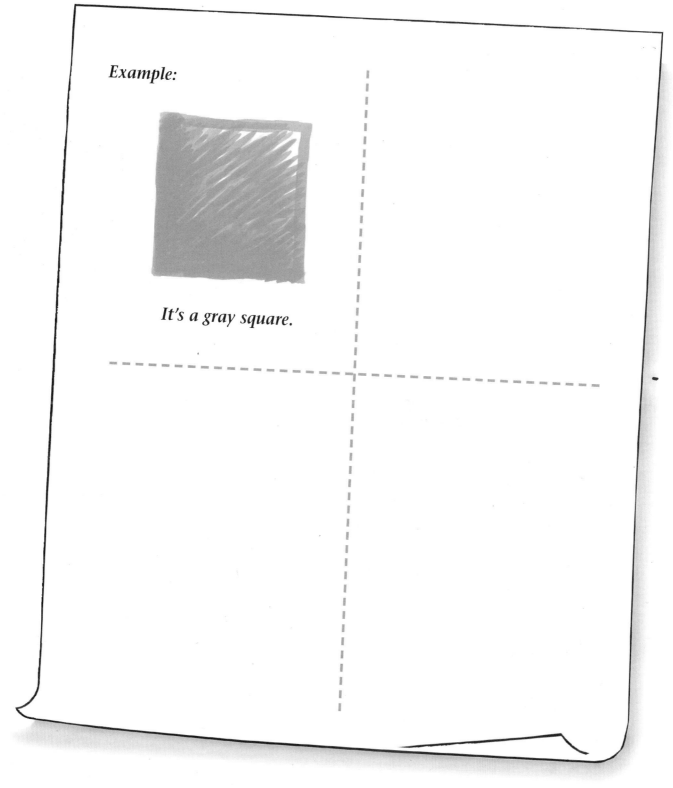

Example:

It's a gray square.

UNIT 3: WHERE WE LIVE
PART 1   THE HOUSE AND YARD   Pages 18–19
Word Power

Write the Picture

Look at the picture of the house and yard. Write the words next to each number.

1. _____

2. _____

3. _____

4. _____

5. _____

6. _____

7. _____

8. _____

9. _____

10. _____

Where is Dusty's bone?
It's in the **flower bed**.

Grammar Box

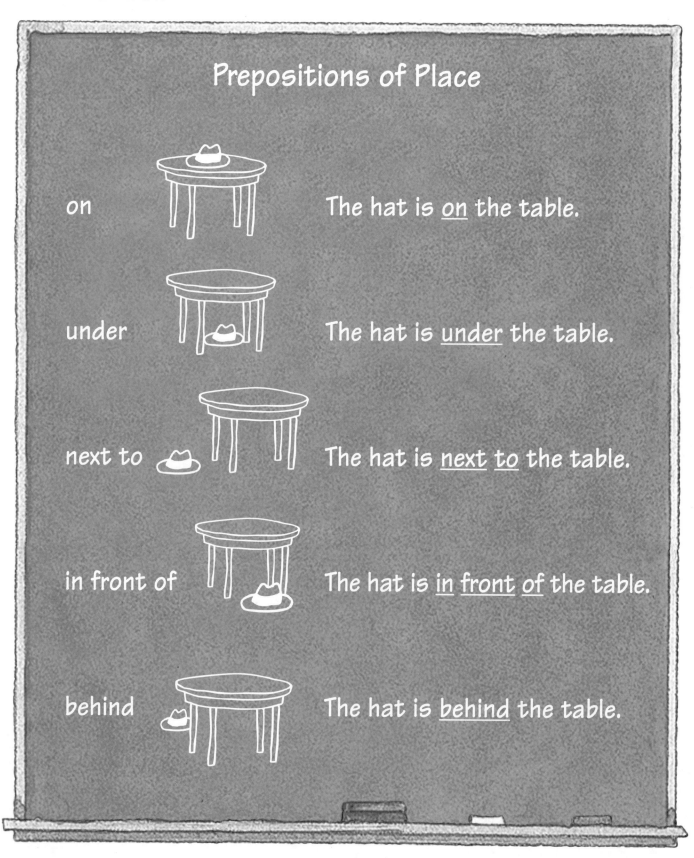

Prepositions of Place

on		The hat is <u>on</u> the table.
under		The hat is <u>under</u> the table.
next to		The hat is <u>next</u> <u>to</u> the table.
in front of		The hat is <u>in</u> <u>front</u> <u>of</u> the table.
behind		The hat is <u>behind</u> the table.

Student Workbook

True or False?

Look at the picture on pages 18–19 in your *Picture Dictionary*.
Write **T** for true and **F** for false.

Example: **Dusty, the dog, is under the tree.** _____F_____

1. The patio chair is in front of the house. _____

2. The lounge chair is next to the umbrella. _____

3. The mailbox is behind the gate. _____

4. The hose is under the window. _____

5. Dusty is on the grass. _____

6. The lawnmower is next to the bicycles. _____

7. The picnic table is behind the house. _____

8. The barbecue is in front of the house. _____

9. The bicycles are on the porch. _____

Word Power

Where is Dusty's bone?
It's in the **flower bed**.

Got It!

Look at the picture on pages 18–19 in your *Picture Dictionary*. Answer the questions, using complete sentences. Use the prepositions of place.

Example: Where is the mailbox? _____*The mailbox is next to the driveway.*_____

1. Where are the birds?

   _____

2. Where is the bench?

   _____

3. Where is the window box?

   _____

4. Where is the townhouse?

   _____

Word Scramble

Unscramble the words.

1. rgeaga _g_ ___ ___ ___ ___ ___

2. thstreu _s_ ___ ___ ___ ___ ___ ___

3. albmeurl _u_ ___ ___ ___ ___ ___ ___ ___

4. dwnwoi _w_ ___ ___ ___ ___ ___

5. ynhcmei _c_ ___ ___ ___ ___ ___

6. obilmxa _m_ ___ ___ ___ ___ ___

7. naprtamet _a_ ___ ___ ___ ___ ___ ___ ___ ___

8. hpcro _p_ ___ ___ ___ ___

Spell It!

Fill in the missing letters. Then write the word.

1. p___ ___ io _____

2. wi ___ ___ ow _____

3. st ___ ___ ___ s _____

4. fen ___ ___ _____

5. r ___ ___ f _____

PART 2   LIVING ROOM AND DINING ROOM Pages 20–21
Word Power

Write the Picture: Living Room

Look at the picture of the living room. Write the words next to each number.

1. _____

2. _____

3. _____

4. _____

5. _____

6. _____

7. _____

8. _____

9. _____

10. _____

Anna, what are you doing?
I'm **washing the dishes.**

Write the Picture: Dining Room

Look at the picture of the dining room. Write the words next to each number.

1. _____

2. _____

3. _____

4. _____

5. _____

6. _____

7. _____

8. _____

9. _____

10. _____

Word Groups

Circle the words that don't belong.

Example:	VCR	*photographs*	stereo	speaker
1.	serving fork	remote control	salad tongs	soup ladle
2.	floor pillow	dining table	hutch	buffet
3.	couch	highchair	candle	armchair
4.	magazines	photographs	books	tablecloth

Listen In

Listen and Point

Look at the picture of the living room on page 20 in your *Picture Dictionary*. Point as you listen.

Anna,
what are you doing?
I'm **washing the dishes**.

Listen and Write

Listen to the dialogues. Complete the sentences.

1. I'm washing the _____ .

2. I'm washing the _____ .

3. I'm washing the _____ .

4. I'm washing the _____ .

5. I'm washing the _____ .

6. I'm washing the _____ .

7. I'm washing the _____ .

PART 3   BEDROOM AND BATHROOM   Pages 22–23

Word Power

Anna, what do you need to buy?
I need to buy a **bath towel**.

Make a Choice

Look at the picture. Write the word. Practice with a partner.

1 4

2

5

3 6

7

1. I need to buy a _____.

2. I need to buy a _____.

3. I need to buy some _____.

4. I need to buy a _____.

5. I need to buy a _____.

6. I need to buy an _____.

7. I need to buy a _____.

Where Do You Find It?

Read the word. Where do you find it? Write **bathroom** or **bedroom**.

Example: nightstand _____*bedroom*_____

1. pillow _____

2. dresser _____

3. faucet _____

4. sheets _____

5. soap _____

6. toothpaste _____

7. toilet _____

8. teddy bear _____

9. bathtub _____

10. blanket _____

11. shampoo _____

12. towel rack _____

13. hanger _____

14. sink _____

Letter List

Look at the pictures on pages 22–23 in your *Picture Dictionary.* Find the words that begin with **S** and **T**. Write the words under the letter.

S	T
shelf	

Listen In

Listen and Decide: Bedroom

Look at the picture of the bedroom above.
Check **True** or **False** as you listen.

1. True _____ False _____

2. True _____ False _____

3. True _____ False _____

4. True _____ False _____

5. True _____ False _____

Bathroom

Look at the picture of the bathroom above.
Check **True** or **False** as you listen.

6. True _____ False _____

7. True _____ False _____

8. True _____ False _____

9. True _____ False _____

10. True _____ False _____

Listen and Check

Anna is talking to her grandmother. Listen to Anna. What does she need to buy?
Check off the words.

1. bath towel _____

2. hand towel _____

3. soap _____

4. shampoo _____

5. blinds _____

6. hair dryer _____

7. alarm clock _____

8. bedspread _____

9. sheets _____

10. pillow _____

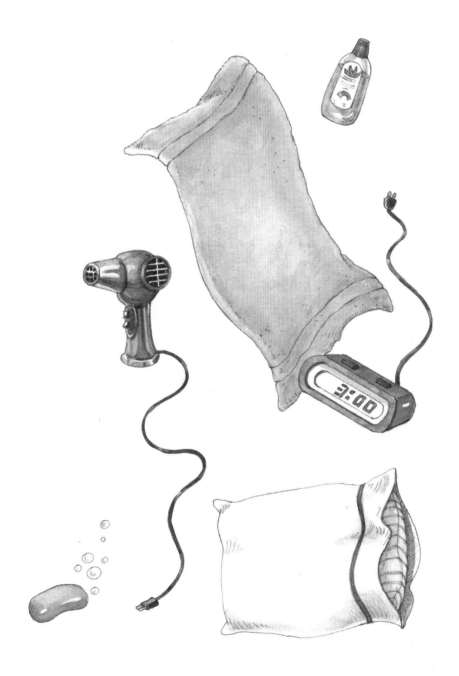

PART 4   KITCHEN AND VERBS   Pages 24–25
Word Power

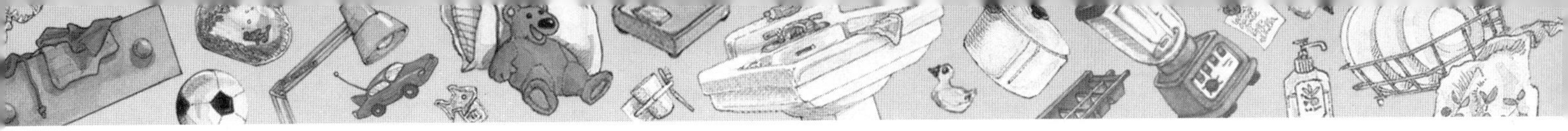

Write the Picture: Kitchen

Look at the picture of the kitchen. Write the words next to each number.

1. _____

2. _____

3. _____

4. _____

5. _____

6. _____

7. _____

8. _____

9. _____

10. _____

Anna, what are you doing?
I'm **cleaning the refrigerator**.

Write the Picture

Look at the picture. Complete the dialogue.
Practice with your partner.

1. What are you doing?

   I'm _____

   _____

2. What are you doing?

   I'm _____

   _____

Student Workbook

3. What are you doing?

I'm _____

_____

4. What are you doing?

I'm _____

_____

5. What are you doing?

I'm _____

_____

6. What are you doing?

I'm _____

_____

Circle the Picture

Read the words. Circle the correct picture for each number.

Example: microwave oven

1. kitchen utensils

3. paper towels

2. hot pad

4. ice tray

Matching

Find the missing words. Write them on the lines.

1. cleaning _____

2. turning off _____

3. walking _____

4. ringing _____

5. opening _____

6. knocking _____

the doorbell

the bedroom

the door

the lights

on the door

downstairs

Listen In

Listen and Point

Look at page 24 in your *Picture Dictionary*. Point to the picture as you listen.

Listen and Check

Listen to the dialogues. Check off the correct words.

1. sink _____   stove _____

2. frying pan _____   freezer _____

3. blender _____   toaster _____

4. rice cooker _____   electric mixer _____

5. dishwasher _____   drawer _____

6. cabinet _____   counter _____

7. cupboard _____   dish rack _____

8. can opener _____   kitchen utensils _____

Looking at Your Life
Draw and Tell

Draw a picture of a room in your house. Draw yourself in the picture. Tell your partner about your picture.

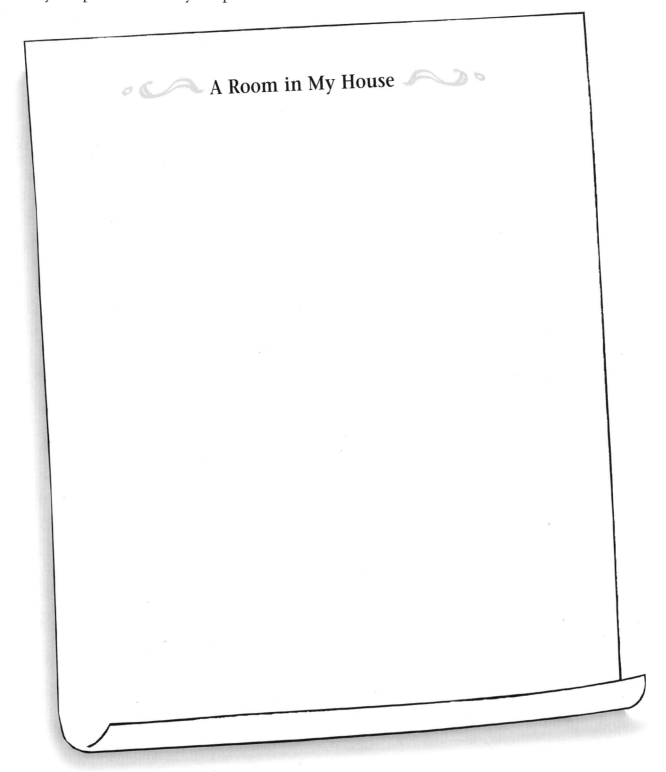

A Room in My House

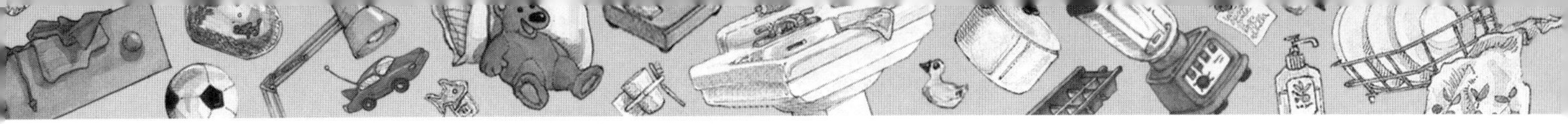

Write It!

Look at your picture from "Draw and Tell." Write about your picture.
Use the words from Unit 3 in your *Picture Dictionary*.

About My Room

This is my _____. I have

a/an_____, a/an_____, and

a/an _____ in my _____.

The _____ is next to

the _____.

I need to buy _____.

Can you see me? I'm _____

_____.

UNIT 4: HOW WE LOOK AND FEEL
PART 1 THE BODY Page 26
Word Power

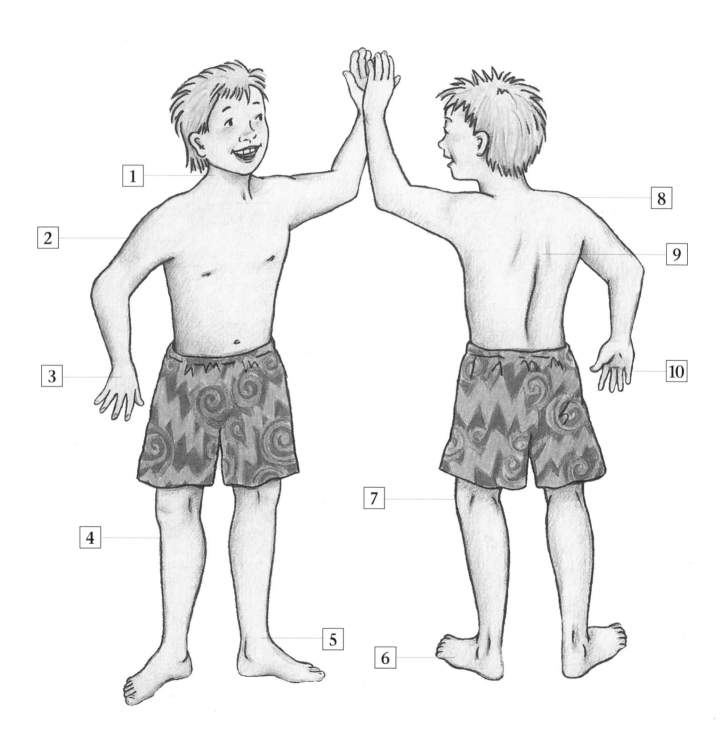

Write the Picture

Look at the pictures of the boy. Write the words for each number.

1. _____   6. _____

2. _____   7. _____

3. _____   8. _____

4. _____   9. _____

5. _____   10. _____

Guess the Word

Look at page 26 in your *Picture Dictionary*. Find the answers.

1. You hear with this. It begins with **e**.

   _____

2. You sit on this. It begins with **b**.

   _____

3. You eat with this. It begins with **m**.

   _____

4. You see with this. It begins with **e**.

   _____

5. You smell with this. It begins with **n**.

   _____

Word Groups

Circle the word that doesn't belong.

1.	cheek	eye	nose	chest
2.	calf	forehead	chin	teeth
3.	ear	thumb	lips	eye
4.	toe	foot	nose	heel
5.	stomach	lips	teeth	tongue
6.	wrist	shoulder	elbow	waist

Word Find

Find the words. Circle the words.

s	b	f	z	h	e	a	d	t	l
h	a	i	r	t	k	l	e	e	s
o	t	g	c	*e*	t	s	r	e	t
u	k	k	h	w	*l*	t	b	t	m
l	s	u	i	r	p	*b*	c	h	a
d	o	y	s	i	w	l	*o*	f	w
e	r	b	u	s	d	g	d	*w*	c
r	w	d	m	t	m	o	q	s	d

elbow

hair

head

shoulder

teeth

wrist

Listen In

What's the matter Tom?
My **arm** hurts.

Listen and Write

Listen to the tape. Write the words for the aches and pains.

1. What's the matter, Susan?

    My _____ hurts.

2. What's the matter, Tom?

    My _____ hurts.

3. What's the matter, Jim?

    My _____ hurts.

4. What's the matter, Bobby?

    My _____ hurts.

5. What's the matter, Anna?

    My _____ hurts.

6. What's the matter, Kate?

    My _____ hurts.

7. What's the matter, David?

    My _____ hurts.

8. What's the matter, Tom?

    My _____ hurts

9. What's the matter, Anna?

    My _____ hurts.

10. What's the matter, Bobby?

    My _____ hurts.

PART 2 DESCRIBING PEOPLE Page 27

Word Power

Opposites

Write the opposite for each word.

1. adult _____*child*_____   5. curly _____

2. beautiful _____   6. male _____

3. short _____   7. fat _____

4. woman _____   8. strong _____

Write the Picture

Look at the pictures. Write a sentence about each picture.

Example: _____*She's beautiful.*_____

1. _____ .

2. _____ .

3. _____ .

4. _____ .

Word Scramble

Unscramble the words.

1. tfabeluiu   __b__ ___ ___ ___ ___ ___ ___ ___ ___

2. grtisaht   __s__ ___ ___ ___ ___ ___ ___ ___

4. gnuyo   __y__ ___ ___ ___ ___

5. lfamee   __f__ ___ ___ ___ ___ ___

Looking at Your Life

What does Bobby's cousin look like?
She's **tall** with **short, blonde hair.**

Write Time

Complete the sentences about people you know. Tell your partner.

1. My mother is _____ with _____, _____ hair.

2. My father is _____ with _____, _____ hair.

3. My teacher is _____ with _____, _____ hair.

4. My best friend is _____ with _____, _____ hair.

Write It!

Write about yourself. Choose the words that describe you.
Tell your partner about yourself.

About Me

I am a _____.

(*boy / girl / man / woman*)

I am _____ and _____

(*tall / short / small / big*)   (*strong / weak / thin / fat*)

with _____, _____,

(*long / short*)   (*straight / curly / wavy*)

_____ hair.

(*black / blonde / brown / gray*)

PART 3   FEELINGS, ACHES, AND PAINS   Pages 28–29

Word Power

Write the Picture

Look at the picture. Write the correct word for the feeling.

1. _____

2. _____

3. _____

4. _____

5. _____

6. _____

7. _____

8. _____

Write the Picture

Look at the picture.
Match the picture to the words.

a. rash	**f.** earache
b. stomach – ache	**g.** sprained wrist
c. twisted ankle	**h.** sunburn
d. *backache*	**i.** headache
e. swollen	**j.** broken arm

Example:

_____ *d*

1. _____

4. _____

7. _____

2. _____

5. _____

8. _____

3. _____

6. _____

9. _____

Student Workbook

Grammar Box

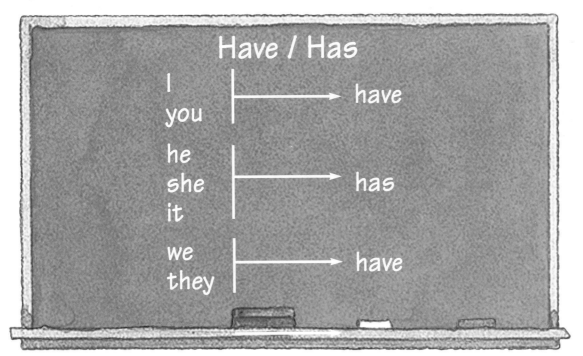

Fill in the Blanks

Write **have** or **has** in the sentence.

1. She _____ a sore throat.

2. They _____ insect bites on their arms.

3. I _____ a cavity in my tooth.

4. He _____ a bad headache.

5. You _____ a sunburn on your face.

6. We _____ bruises on our knees.

Listen In

How do you feel?
I'm **surprised**.

What's wrong?
I'm **worried**.

Listen and Write

Listen to the tape. Write the feeling.

1. Susan: I'm _____ .

2. Karen: I'm _____ .

3. Dave: I'm _____ .

4. Jill: I'm _____ .

5. Cathy: I'm _____ .

6. Tom: I'm _____ .

7. Peter: I'm _____ .

8. Sarah: I'm _____ .

9. Donna: I'm _____ .

10. Rick: I'm _____ .

Listen and Point

Look at page 29 in your *Picture Dictionary*. Listen to the tape.
Point to the picture as you listen.

Listen and Write

Listen to the tape. Write the aches and pains.

1. My head hurts. I have a _____.

2. My tooth hurts. I have a _____ .

3. My back hurts. I have a _____.

4. My finger hurts. I have a _____.

5. My skin hurts. I have a _____.

6. My skin itches. I have a _____.

7. My throat hurts. I have a _____.

8. My ear hurts. I have an _____.

9. My wrist hurts. I have a _____.

10. My ankle hurts. I have a _____.

Listen and Match

Listen to the dialogues. Write the aches and pains next to the name.

EXAMPLE: *Carol:* _____*headache*_____

1. Joe: _____

2. Bob: _____

3. Mrs. Sims: _____

4. Jane: _____

5. Joe: _____

6. Jimmy: _____

Listen and Decide

Listen to the dialogue. Write **T** for true. Write **F** for false.

1. Bobby is ill. _____

2. Bobby is cold. _____

3. Bobby is tired. _____

4. Bobby has a headache. _____

5. Bobby has a cough. _____

6. Bobby has an earache. _____

7. Bobby has a sore throat. _____

PART 4 VERBS Pages 30–31
Word Power

Letter List
Write the verbs from page 30 in your *Picture Dictionary* under the letter.

B

_____

_____

_____

D

_____

_____

_____

S

_____

_____

_____

_____

W

_____

_____

_____

_____

Matching

Circle the words that match the pictures.

1.

crying

laughing

5.

kicking

throwing

2.

getting dressed

getting undressed

6.

drinking

talking

3.

taking a bath

taking a shower

7.

going to bed

getting up

4.

drying your hands

washing your hands

8.

jumping

walking

Head, Mouth, Arms, and Legs

Circle the verbs that *don't* match the pictures.

1. HEAD

listening

playing

talking

thinking

3. ARMS

kissing

throwing

waving

pointing

2. MOUTH

eating

crying

biting

drinking

4. LEGS

jumping

kicking

dancing

laughing

Got It!

Read the sentence. Complete the sentence using a verb.

1. I'm hungry. I'm _____ *eating* _____ .

2. I'm sad. I'm _____ .

3. I hear music. I'm _____ .

4. I'm thirsty. I'm _____ .

5. I'm tired. I'm _____ .

6. It's funny. I'm _____ .

7. My hair is dirty. I'm _____ .

8. I'm happy. I'm _____ .

9. It's morning. I'm _____ .

10. My hands are wet. I'm _____ .

The Five Senses

Write the sense next to the part of the body.

1. nose _____

2. ears _____

3. tongue _____

4. fingers _____

5. eyes _____

Student Workbook

What's the Sense?

Circle any words that match the sense.

1. TASTING

soup

cheek

sweet

mouth

flower

3. SMELLING

smoke

rose

laughing

cold

sneezing

2. HEARING

ocean

food

music

sun

listening

4. TOUCHING

soft

hand

pointing

warm

nauseous

5. SEEING

earphones

picture

talking

TV

sky

Looking at Your Life
Draw and Tell

Draw a picture of yourself. What do you look like? How do you feel today? Draw it.
Show your partner. Tell your partner about yourself.

About Myself

My name is _____ .

I am _____ with _____ _____ hair.

Today I am _____ . I feel _____ .

Write It!

Look at the pictures. Describe the people.

Example:

He is a man.

He is tall with short brown hair.

He is tired.

He is standing

1. _____

   _____

   _____

   _____

2. _____

   _____

   _____

   _____

UNIT 5: PEOPLE WE KNOW Pages 32–35

Who is Anna's
grandmother?
Mary is Anna's
grandmother.

Write the Picture

Read the dialogue box. Look at pages 32–33 in your *Picture Dictionary* and answer the questions with complete sentences.

Example: Who is Anna's mom? ___*Donna is Anna's mom.*___

1. Who is Anna's dad? _____

_____

2. Who is Anna's brother? _____

_____

3. Who is Anna's sister? _____

_____

4. Who is Anna's grandpa? _____

_____

5. Who is Anna's grandma? _____

_____

6. Who is Anna's aunt? _____

_____

7. Who is Anna's uncle? _____

_____

8. Who is Anna's female cousin? _____

_____

Fill in the Chart

Read the words below. Which are male? Which are female? Write the words in the correct side of the chart.

grandpa	sister	aunt
uncle	mother	dad
grandmother	brother	cousin

Male	Female
grandpa	

Fill in the Blanks

Look at pages 32-35 in your *Picture Dictionary*. Fill in the blanks.

sister	brother	best friend	pet
uncle	mom	grandpa	

1. Joe is Anna's _____.

2. Dusty is Anna's _____.

3. Cathy is Anna's _____.

4. Lee is Anna's _____.

5. Donna is Anna's _____.

6. Ben is Anna's _____.

Word Scramble

This is Anna's family. Read the clues. Use the clues to unscramble the words.

1. father's father

   daapgrn _g_ ___ ___ ___ ___ ___ ___

2. aunt's daughter

   scniuo _c_ ___ ___ ___ ___ ___

3. father's mother

   dnghomreatr _g_ ___ ___ ___ ___ ___ ___ ___ ___ ___ ___

4. father's sister

   tanu _a_ ___ ___ ___

5. mother's brother

   enlcu _u_ ___ ___ ___ ___

True and False

Look at pages 32–35 in your *Picture Dictionary*. Then read the sentences.
Write **T** for true. Write **F** for false.

1. Joe is Anna's brother. _____

2. Ben is Anna's father. _____

3. Cathy is Anna's best friend. _____

4. Anna has two cousins. _____

5. Dusty is Anna's pet. _____

6. Anna's grandmother is Craig's neighbor. _____

7. Cathy is Craig's girlfriend. _____

Listen In

Listen and Point

Listen to the tape. Point to the people on pages 34–35 in your *Picture Dictionary*.

Listen and Write

Listen to the tape. Write the names.

1. _____

2. _____

3. _____

4. _____

5. _____

6. _____

7. _____

8. _____

9. _____

Listen and Spell

Listen to the words. Spell the words.

1. _____

2. _____

3. _____

4. _____

5. _____

6. _____

Student Workbook

Grammar Box

Possessive Nouns

the mother of Anna = Anna's mother

the friend
of my mother = my mother's
friend

Fill in the Blanks

Read the sentences. Write the possessive nouns.

1. John is the son of Mary. John is _____ son.

2. Anna is the sister of Cathy. Anna is _____ sister.

3. Joe is the son of John. Joe is _____ son.

4. Bobby is the brother of Jane. Bobby is _____ brother.

5. Ben is the father of Jane. Ben is _____ father.

6. Sam is the grandfather of Cathy. Sam is _____ grandfather.

7. Donna is the mother of Joe. Donna is _____ mother.

8. Jane is the daughter of Kim. Jane is _____ daughter.

Looking at Your Life

Draw and Tell

Draw your family tree. Write the names. Show your partner.

Example:

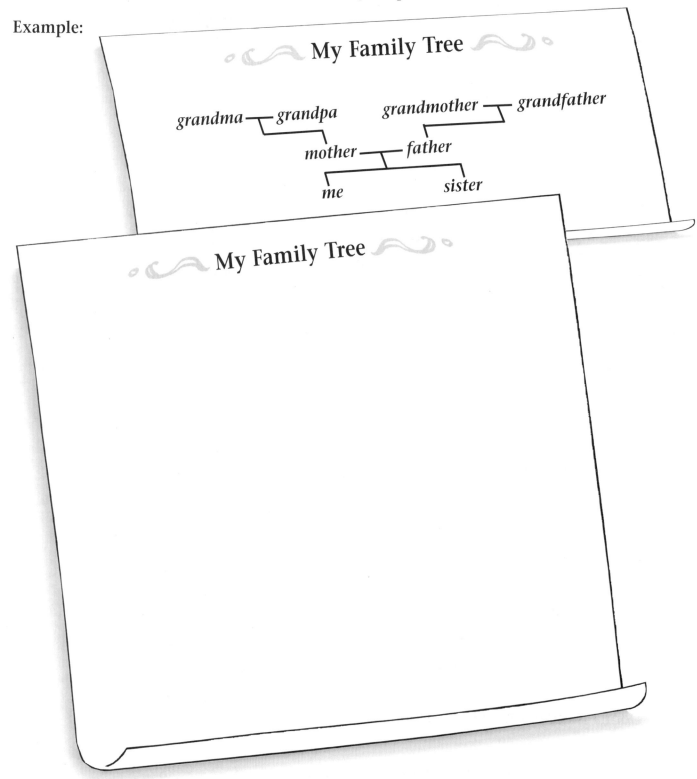

My Family Tree

grandma —— grandpa   grandmother —— grandfather

mother —— father

me   sister

My Family Tree

Write It!

Write a story about your family. Use your family tree and the words from pages 32-35 in your *Picture Dictionary*.

Example:

My Family

This is my family. Mary is my mother. She is tall with blonde hair. Ted is my father. He is tall with black hair. Lori is my sister. She is tall with brown hair. My Aunt Elaine is my father's sister. Harry is my pet.

My Family

_____

_____

_____

_____

_____

_____

_____

_____

UNIT 6: FOODS WE EAT
PART 1   VEGETABLES AND FRUITS   Pages 36–37

Word Power
Write the Picture

Look at the pictures. Write the words.

Vegetables	Fruits
1. _____	1. _____
2. _____	2. _____
3. _____	3. _____

Vegetables	Fruits
4. _____	4. _____
5. _____	5. _____
6. _____	6. _____

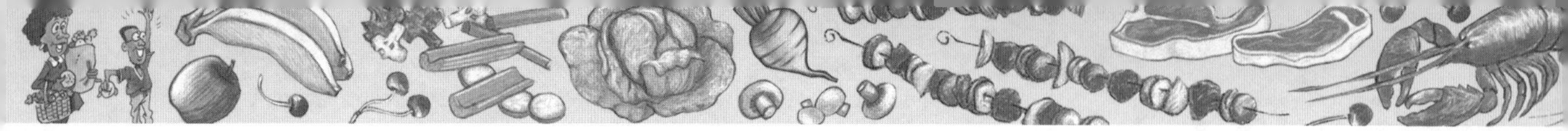

Letter List

Look at the pictures on pages 36–37 in your *Picture Dictionary*. Find the words that start with **A**, **B**, **C**, and **P**. Write the words under the letters.

A

_____

_____

_____

_____

B

_____

_____

_____

_____

C

_____

_____

_____

_____

_____

P

_____

_____

_____

_____

_____

Listen In

Listen and Point

Listen to the tape. Point to the pictures on pages 36–37 in your *Picture Dictionary*.

Do you like **berries**?
Yes, I do.

Listen and Check

Listen to the dialogues. What does Anna like to eat? Check the vegetables and fruits that she likes.

1. grapes _____

2. mangos _____

3. squash _____

4. plums _____

5. berries _____

6. carrots _____

7. kiwis _____

8. turnips _____

9. corn _____

10. bananas _____

11. pears _____

12. lettuce _____

13. artichokes _____

14. cabbage _____

15. apricots _____

16. mushrooms _____

PART 2   MEAT, POULTRY, AND SEAFOOD   Pages 38–39

Word Power

Would you like **chicken** or **turkey**?
I'd like **turkey** please.

Write the picture

Look at the pictures. Complete the dialogues. Answer the questions with your choice.

Example:

   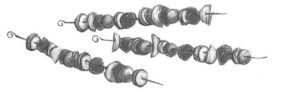

Would you like _____ *steak* _____ or _____ *kebobs* _____?

I'd like _____ *steak* _____ please.

1. Would you like _____ or _____?

I'd like _____ please.

Student Workbook

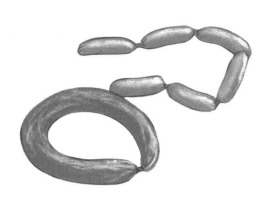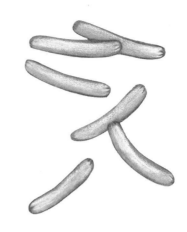

2. Would you like _____ or_____?

I'd like _____ please.

3. Would you like _____ or _____?

I'd like _____ please.

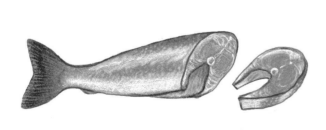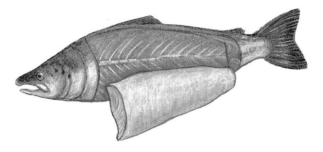

4. Would you like _____ or _____?

I'd like _____ please.

Fill in the Chart

Look at pages 38–39 in your *Picture Dictionary*. Write the words in the correct boxes.

ribs	kebobs	sausage	bologna	crab
bacon	oysters	duck	chicken	steak
lobster	liverwurst	hamburger	lamb chops	
salami	turkey	ham	leg of lamb	

Beef	Lamb	Pork
_____	_____	_____
_____	_____	_____
_____	_____	_____

Cold Cuts	Poultry	Seafood
_____	_____	_____
_____	_____	_____
_____	_____	_____

Listen In

Listen and Spell

Listen to the tape. Spell the words.

1. _____

2. _____

3. _____

4. _____

5. _____

6. _____

7. _____

8. _____

9. _____

10. _____

Listen and Write

Listen to the dialogues. What do the people want? Write the choice for each person.

1. Anna: _____

2. Tim: _____

3. Bobby: _____

4. Jimmy: _____

5. Katie: _____

6. Susan: _____

7. Robin: _____

8. Tom: _____

PART 3 DAIRY FOODS AND GRAINS, BEVERAGES, SNACKS AND DESSERTS Pages 40–41

Word Power
Write the Picture
Look at the pictures. Check the correct words.

1. crackers _____

   bagels _____

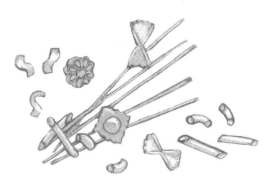

4. cereal _____

   pasta _____

2. butter _____

   cheese _____

5. muffins _____

   rolls _____

3. pie _____

   ice cream _____

6. tea _____

   coffee _____

Student Workbook

Do you want some **breadsticks**?
Yes, please.

Word Groups

Circle the words that don't belong.

1.	milk	cheese	cream	rice
2.	eggs	popcorn	dried fruit	nuts
3.	cake	pie	cereal	cookies
4.	milkshake	butter	lemonade	iced tea
5.	yogurt	rolls	muffins	bagels

Grammar Box

Quantifiers

a   before consonants (all letters except vowels) example: *a pretzel*

an   before vowels (a,e,i,o,u) example: *an apple*

a/an   with singular-count nouns example: *a pretzel, an apple*

some   with plural-count nouns example: *some pretzels, some apples*

and, with all non-count nouns example: *some tea, some coffee*

Fill in the Blanks

Fill in the blanks. Use **a**, **an**, or **some**.

1. Do you want _____ rice cakes?

2. Do you want _____ egg?

3. Do you want _____ apple?

4. Do you want _____ carrot?

5. Do you want _____ coffee?

6. Do you want _____ cookies?

7. Do you want _____ orange?

8. Do you want _____ cereal?

PART 4   MEALTIME   Pages 42–43

Word Power
What's the Meal?

Write **B** for breakfast. Write **L** for lunch. Write **D** for dinnner.
Write **S** for snack. Write **DE** for dessert.

1. waffles _____

2. sandwich _____

3. potato chips _____

4. cake _____

5. steak _____

6. muffin _____

7. fried chicken _____

8. hot dog _____

9. ice cream _____

10. pasta with vegetables _____

11. hot cereal _____

12. soup _____

13. hamburger and french fries _____

14. yogurt and fruit _____

15. dried fruit _____

16. popcorn _____

Listen In
Listen and Choose

Listen to the tape. Circle the correct pictures.

1.

2.

3.

4.

Student Workbook

5.

6.

7.

8.

9.

10.

Looking at Your Life
Draw and Tell

What foods do you like? Draw your favorite foods in the chart.

Ask your partner: "Do you like _____?"

Vegetables	Fruits
Dairy Foods and Grains	**Snacks and Desserts**

Write It!

Fill in the blanks with the words from "Draw and Tell."

My Favorite Foods

My favorite foods are _____,

_____, and _____.

For breakfast, I like to eat _____.

For lunch, I like to eat _____

and _____.

For dinner, I like to eat _____

and _____.

My favorite dessert is _____.

UNIT 7: WHAT WE WEAR Pages 44–47

Word Power
Write the Picture
Look at the pictures. Write the words.

1. _____

4. _____

2. _____

5. _____

3. _____

6. _____

Student Workbook

7. _____

10. _____

8. _____

11. _____

9. _____

12. _____

Feet, Legs, and Arms

Look at the list of words. Write the words for the clothing under the correct body parts.

loafers	high heels	pants
slacks	tee shirt	shoes
stockings	jeans	sweatpants
long-sleeved shirt	sweater	sneakers
tights	sweatshirt	socks

Feet

Legs

Arms

_____

_____

_____

_____

_____

Student Workbook

Make a Choice

Choose the clothing for each activity. Circle any words that are correct.

1. **SCHOOL**

   pajamas

   book bag

   bathing suit

4. **RAIN**

   umbrella

   undershirt

   sandals

2. **SLEEP**

   stockings

   skirt

   pajamas

5. **SPORTS**

   sneakers

   blouse

   slacks

3. **OFFICE**

   suit

   sneakers

   shorts

6. **BEACH**

   coat

   nightgown

   sandals

Choose the Word

Look at the pictures. Read the words. Write the correct words under the pictures.

Example: hat

               cap

            hat   *cap*
_____   _____

1. wristwatch

     bracelet

_____   _____

2. tie

    belt

_____   _____

Student Workbook

3. backpack

briefcase

_____   _____

4. wallet

purse

_____   _____

5. earrings

ring

_____   _____

I like your new **cap**, Jim.
Thanks.

Word Groups

Circle the words that do not belong.

1.	backpack	cap	book bag	briefcase
2.	jacket	slacks	jeans	sweatpants
3.	boots	sandals	tights	loafers
4.	undershirt	boxers	bathing suit	slip
5.	earrings	necklace	ring	umbrella

Student Workbook

Grammar Box

Like / Likes

I
we → like
they

she → likes
he

Fill in the Blanks

Read the sentences. Fill in the blank with **like** or **likes**.

1. She _____ her new hat.

2. We _____ our new sneakers.

3. They _____ their new sweatpants.

4. He _____ his new tie.

5. I _____ my new bathing suit.

Listen In
Listen and Spell

Listen to the tape. Write the words.

1. _____

2. _____

3. _____

4. _____

5. _____

6. _____

7. _____

8. _____

9. _____

10. _____

11. _____

12. _____

Listen and Choose

Listen to the tape. Choose the correct words.

1. underwear _____   undershirt _____

2. long-sleeved shirt _____   short-sleeved shirt _____

3. blouse _____   boots _____

4. sweatpants _____   sweatshirt _____

5. pants _____   slacks _____

6. book bag _____   backpack _____

7. ring _____   earrings _____

Listen and Decide

Listen to the conversations. Write **T** for true or **F** for false.

1. Susan has a new hat. _____

2. Jim has a new tie. _____

3. Anna has a new coat. _____

4. Tom has a new book bag. _____

5. Kate has a new tee-shirt. _____

6. Susan has a new dress. _____

7. Anna has new stockings. _____

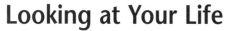

Looking at Your Life
Draw and Tell

You just went shopping. Draw your new clothing, jewelry, and accessories. Look at your partner's drawing. Practice using the dialogue on page 47 in your *Picture Dictionary*.

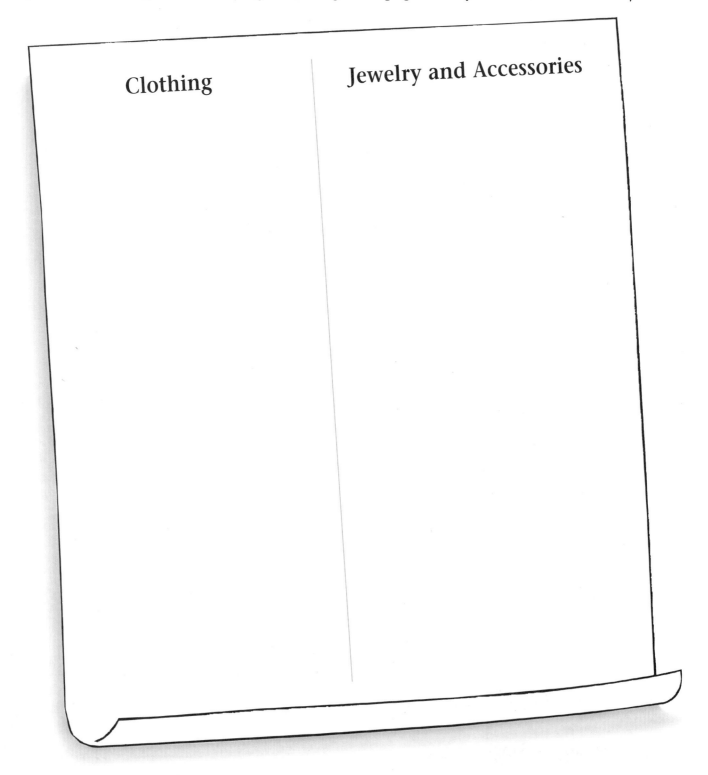

Clothing

Jewelry and Accessories

Write It!

Write about your day at the beach. Choose one of the words for each of the blanks.

~ My Day at the Beach ~

Today I'm at the beach. I have my _____
(bathing suit / underwear)

and _____. I also have my
(boots / sandals)

_____ and _____.
(shorts / slacks)   (tank top / suit)

I don't have my _____
(cap / tie)

or _____.
(book bag / wristwatch)

If it gets cold, I have my _____
(sweatshirt / coat)

and _____.
(socks / stockings)

UNIT 8: OUR INTERESTS Pages 48–51

Word Power

Write the Picture: Indoor Activities

Look at the pictures. What are they doing? Write the activities.

1. _____

2. _____

3. _____

4. _____

5. _____

6. _____

7. _____

8. _____

9. _____

10. _____

Matching: Music

Find the matching pictures. Write the letters on the lines.

Example: country music _____*h*_____

1. classical music _____

2. blues _____

3. folk music _____

4. jazz _____

5. rock n'roll _____

6. pop music _____

7. opera _____

Word Scramble: Music

Unscramble the words. Write the words on the lines.

1. srmud _d_ ___ ___ ___ ___

   _____

2. tiragu _g_ ___ ___ ___ ___ ___

   _____

3. zajz _j_ ___ ___ ___

   _____

4. nopshoxae _s_ ___ ___ ___ ___ ___ ___ ___ ___

   _____

5. tuprmet _t_ ___ ___ ___ ___ ___ ___

   _____

Circle the Picture

Look at the pictures. Circle the pictures that match the words.

1. aerobics

2. frisbee

3. wrestling

4. badminton

5. diving

Student Workbook

Matching

Look at pages 50–51 in your *Picture Dictionary*. Find the sports equipment for each sport. Write the words on the lines.

Sports	Sports Equipment
tennis	*tennis racket, tennis ball*
hockey	
cycling	
swimming	
baseball	
football	
badminton	
ice skating	
table tennis	

What are your favorite sports, Kate?

I like **swimming**, **tennis**, and **cycling**.

Word Groups

Circle the words that don't belong.

1.　soccer　　　　　football

　　swimming　　　baseball

2.　hockey　　　　　ice skating

　　skiing　　　　　surfing

3.　windsurfing　　　badminton

　　tennis　　　　　table tennis

4.　ice skating　　　skateboarding

　　gymnastics　　　in-line skating

Grammar Box

Do / Does

What _do you_ do in _your_ free time?

What _does he_ do in _his_ free time?

What _does she_ do in _her_ free time?

What _do they_ do in _their_ free time?

Fill in the Blanks

Read the sentence. Fill in the blanks with **do** or **does**.

1. What _____ he do in his free time?

2. What _____ you want for breakfast?

3. What _____ she need to buy?

4. What _____ they do after work?

5. What _____ you need to buy?

What do you do in your free time, David?

I like **painting** and **listening to music**.

Listen In

Listen and Point

Listen to the tape. Point to the pictures on pages 48-49 in your *Picture Dictionary*.

Listen and Spell

Listen to the words. Spell the words.

1. _____

2. _____

3. _____

4. _____

5. _____

6. _____

7. _____

Listen and Decide

Listen to the tape again. Write **D** for what David likes.
Write **K** for what Kate likes.

1. reading a book _____

2. playing the saxophone _____

3. sewing _____

4. listening to music _____

5. painting _____

6. watching a video _____

7. knitting _____

8. playing the piano _____

9. woodworking _____

10. calligraphy _____

Looking at Your Life

Draw and Tell

What do you like to do in your free time? Draw your favorite activities and sports. Tell your partner.

Activities

Sports

Write It!

Complete the paragraph. Write about your interests.

My Interests

In my free time, I like _____,

_____, and _____.

My favorite music is _____ and

_____. My favorite sports are

_____, _____,

and _____.

I also like _____

and _____.

UNIT 9: HOW WE MEASURE TIME Pages 52–55

Word Power

Write the Picture

Look at the clocks. Write each time three different ways.

Example:

5:30

five-thirty

half past five

1. _____

_____

_____

2. _____

_____

_____

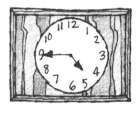

3. _____

_____

_____

4. _____

_____

_____

Fill in the Chart

Read the list of daily activities. Match the activities with the times of day. Write them on the lines.

eating breakfast   sleeping   going to bed

getting undressed   taking a shower   eating lunch

brushing your teeth   eating dinner   going to school

getting dressed   reading a book   playing a video game

Morning	Afternoon	Evening
_____	_____	_____
_____	_____	_____
_____	_____	_____
_____	_____	_____
_____	_____	_____
_____	_____	_____

What time is it?

It's a **quarter after** three.

When do you go to school?

I go to school in the **morning**.

Listen In

Listen and Choose

Listen to the tape. Choose the correct times.

1. 8:15 _____   8:50 _____

2. 3:15 _____   2:45 _____

3. 7:13 _____   7:30 _____

4. 10:15 _____   9:45 _____

5. 7:30 _____   7:00 _____

6. 2:45 _____   3:45 _____

7. 4:00 _____   5:00 _____

8. 1:40 _____   1:30 _____

Listen and Check

Listen to the conversation about Anna's daily activities. Check the times of day.

Activity	Morning	Afternoon	Evening
gets up	_____	_____	_____
takes a shower	_____	_____	_____
goes to school	_____	_____	_____
eats lunch	_____	_____	_____
rides her bicycle	_____	_____	_____
does her homework	_____	_____	_____
goes to bed	_____	_____	_____

What day is it?
It's **Friday**.

Listen and Write

Listen to the tape. Write the day or month.

1. _____

2. _____

3. _____

4. _____

5. _____

6. _____

7. _____

8. _____

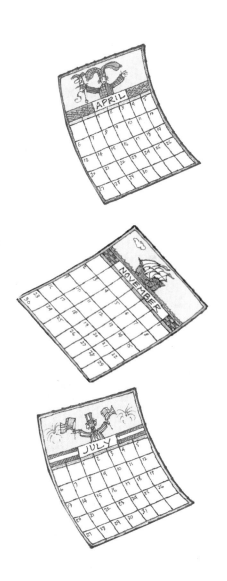

Student Workbook

Grammar Box

Time Words

at   7 o'clock
noon
midnight

on   Monday, Tuesday, Wednesday. . .
the weekend

in   September, October, November. . .
the morning, the afternoon, the evening

Fill in the Blanks

1. Anna goes to school _____ 8 o'clock.

2. Tom takes a shower _____ the morning.

3. Dusty gets a bath _____ the weekend.

4. David eats his lunch _____ noon.

5. Kate's birthday is _____ September.

6. Bobby plays baseball _____ Saturday.

7. Susan plays her flute _____ the afternoon.

Looking at Your Life
Draw and Tell

Draw a clock in each box. Tell your partner about your day.

Get Up	Go to School
Eat Dinner	**Go to Bed**

Write It!

Write about your day. Complete the sentences with time words.

◦ ⌒ ◦ My Day ◦ ⌒ ◦

I get up _____.

I eat breakfast _____.

I go to school _____.

I do my homework _____.

I eat dinner _____.

I go to bed _____.

UNIT 10: THE ENVIRONMENT

PART 1   THE SEASONS AND WEATHER   Pages 56–59

Word Power

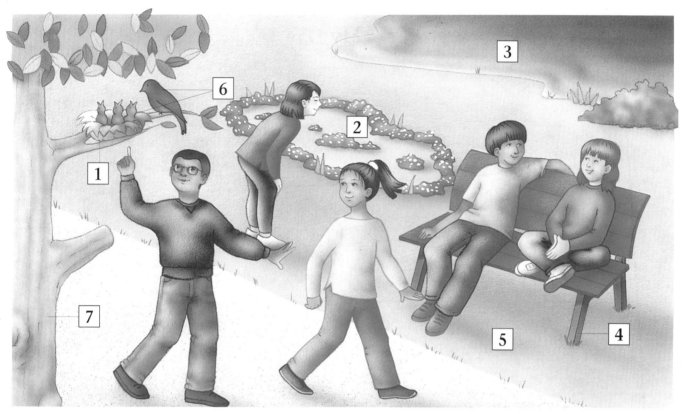

Write the Picture

Look at the picture of Spring. Write the words.

1. _____

2. _____

3. _____

4. _____

5. _____

6. _____

7. _____

Look at the picture of Summer. Write the words.

1. _____

2. _____

3. _____

4. _____

5. _____

6. _____

7. _____

8. _____

Name the Season

Which seasons match the words? Write **SU** for summer and **WI** for winter.

1. swimming _____

2. sled _____

3. ice chest _____

4. watermelon _____

5. snowman _____

6. ice skating _____

7. gloves _____

8. beach _____

9. lifeguard _____

10. ice _____

Word Groups

Circle the words that don't belong.

1.	flowers	cold	bench	nest
2.	leaf	rake	sweater	sand
3.	iced tea	sled	ice skates	snowman
4.	lifeguard	towel	watermelon	gloves
5.	hat	flowers	snow	jacket

Fill in the Chart

Find the words for nice weather. Write them under the happy face. Find the words for bad weather. Write them under the sad face.

sunny	cold	windy
wet	thunder	clear
warm	hail	sunshine
cool	stormy	hazy
hot	snowy	windy

What's the weather like there?

It's **sunny** and **warm**.

Listen In
Listen and Check

Listen to the tape. Check the correct words.

1. sunny _____

   foggy _____

   warm _____

   hot _____

2. cold _____

   snowy _____

   windy _____

   cool _____

3. cold _____

   hazy _____

   hot _____

   warm _____

4. windy _____

   clear _____

   cool _____

   foggy _____

5. stormy _____

   cloudy _____

   wet _____

   cold _____

7. warm _____

   hot _____

   hazy _____

   rainy _____

6. snowy _____

   rainy _____

   windy _____

   wet _____

8. clear _____

   cool _____

   foggy _____

   stormy _____

Listen and Choose

Listen to the tape. Choose the word with the opposite meaning.

1. cloudy _____   windy _____

2. sunny _____   hazy _____

3. cold _____   warm _____

4. snowy _____   cool _____

5. snowy _____   clear _____

PART 2   LAND AND WATER   Pages 60–61
Word Power

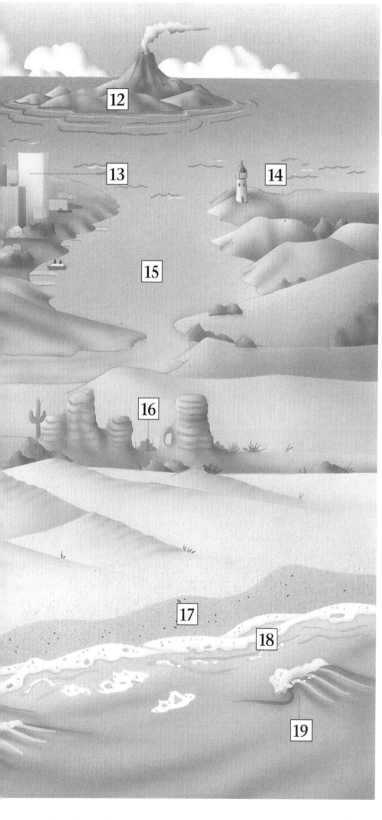

Write the Picture

Look at the pictures. Write the words.

1. _____

2. _____

3. _____

4. _____

5. _____

6. _____

7. _____

8. _____

9. _____

10. _____

11. _____

12. _____

13. _____

14. _____

15. _____

16. _____

17. _____

18. _____

19. _____

Fill in the Chart

Read the word list. Check **Land** or **Water** for each word.

Word List	Land	Water
mountain	_____	_____
bay	_____	_____
river	_____	_____
beach	_____	_____
seashore	_____	_____
ocean	_____	_____
grass	_____	_____
valley	_____	_____
lake	_____	_____
meadow	_____	_____
dune	_____	_____
stream	_____	_____
wave	_____	_____
jungle	_____	_____
hill	_____	_____

Spell It!

Fill in the missing letters. Then write the words.

1. m ___ ___ nt ___ ___ n   _____

2. i ___ la ___ d   _____

3. s ___ ___ e a ___   _____

4. o ___ ___ ___ n   _____

5. s ___ ___ sho ___ ___   _____

6. va ___ ___ e ___   _____

Grammar Box

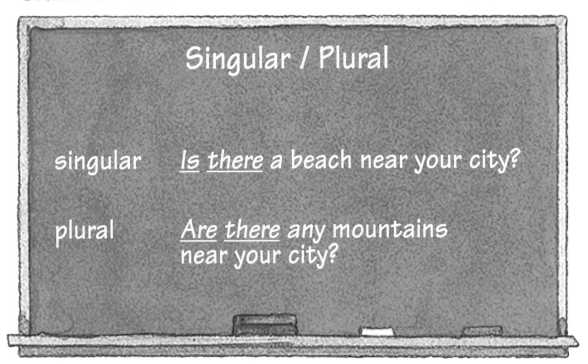

Singular / Plural

singular   _Is there_ a beach near your city?

plural   _Are there_ any mountains near your city?

Fill in the blanks

Read the sentences. Fill in the blanks with **Is there a** or **Are there any**.

1. _____ hills near your city?

2. _____ meadow in your hometown?

3. _____ desert in your country?

4. _____ islands near your city?

5. _____ rivers near your school?

6. _____ seashore near your house?

7. _____ forests near your city?

8. _____ jungle in your country?

Listen In

Listen and Check

Listen to Anna talk about her city. Check either **Yes** or **No** after each word.

1. beaches   Yes _____   No _____   5. jungles   Yes _____   No _____

2. lakes   Yes _____   No _____   6. valleys   Yes _____   No _____

3. mountains   Yes _____   No _____   7. hills   Yes _____   No _____

4. islands   Yes _____   No _____   8. rivers   Yes _____   No _____

Listen and Decide

Listen to Anna talk about her city. Write **T** for true or **F** for false.

1. Anna lives in a small city. _____

2. There are mountains near Anna's city. _____

3. Anna goes ice skating in the autumn. _____

4. There is a meadow near Anna's city. _____

5. In the spring, the meadow is beautiful. _____

6. There are no flowers. _____

7. Anna likes taking a walk in the meadow. _____

8. There is a beach near Anna's city. _____

9. In the summer, she goes swimming in the lake. _____

10. There is a lifeguard at the beach. _____

11. There is a forest near Anna's city. _____

12. In the autumn, it is hot and sunny. _____

13. Anna likes climbing trees in the forest. _____

Looking at Your Life
Draw and Tell

Draw a picture of your favorite season. Tell your partner about your picture.

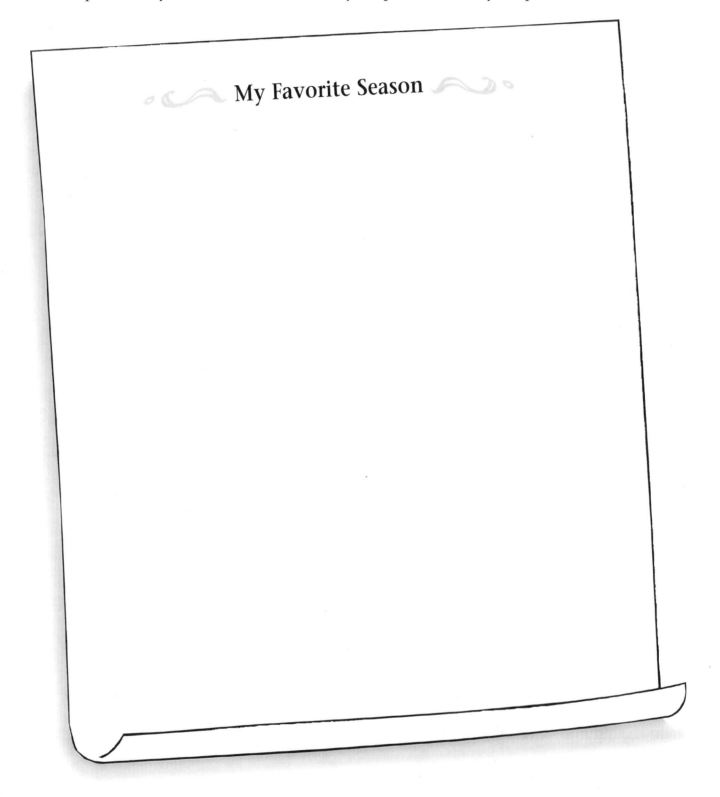

My Favorite Season

Student Workbook

Write It!

Fill in the blanks. Write about your city.

About My City

I live in a _____ . _____ city. There are

_____ , _____ , and

_____ near my city. There is a

_____ near my city too. In the

winter, the weather is _____

and _____ . In the spring, the weather

is _____ and _____ .

In the summer, the weather is _____

and _____ . In the autumn, the weather is

_____ and _____ .

INDEX

Topics

Grammar Points